GW00391235

Silver Link Silk Editions

SLP

One young lad's further trainspotting trips with a camera 1961-1964

One of a class of 422, and with 38 years of service under her belt, this is 3F 'Jinty' No 47454 – her relatively high chimney trying to compete with the one in the right background – doing some shunting in the Skipton yards to build up her final load. (29 July 1964)

Silver Link Silk Editions

SLP

One young lad's further trainspotting trips with a camera 1961-1964

Alan M. Clarke

Silver Link Publishing Ltd

© Alan M. Clarke 2018

All rights reserved. No part of this
publication may be reproduced, stored in a
retrieval system or transmitted, in any form
or by any means, electronic, mechanical,
photocopying, recording or otherwise,
without prior permission in writing from
Silver Link Publishing Ltd.

First published in 2018

British Library Cataloguing in Publication
Data

A catalogue record for this book is
available from the British Library.

ISBN 978 1 85794 514 0

Silver Link Publishing Ltd
The Trundle
Ringstead Road
Great Addington
Kettering
Northants NN14 4BW

Tel/Fax: 01536 330588
email: sales@nostalgiacollection.com
Website: www.nostalgiacollection.com

Printed and bound in the Czech Republic

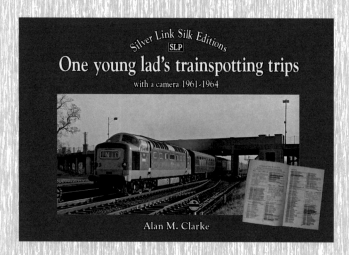

The first volume ISBN: 978 1 85794 472 3

Contents

Dedication

Those we love don't go away
They walk beside us every day
Unseen, unheard but always near
Still loved, still missed and very dear.

Miss you, Chris. Love, Alan xxx

Introduction

Having started trainspotting at ten years of age it quickly became a very important part of my life, together with following Sheffield Wednesday, as a season ticket holder, which meant that every other Saturday during the football season was spent at Hillsborough, with the alternate weekends off trainspotting somewhere. One of my early wishes was to have my own Ian Allan *abc British Railways Locomotives Combined Volume*; priced at 10s 6d, this twice-yearly publication listed all locomotives that were currently operating on the system.

So, having saved up enough money, after school at 3.30pm I used to go down each day to the local Smiths shop and check to see if the Summer 1959 edition of the 'Combined' had arrived. Well, one day the Manager, who knew me by now, called me and said it was in, but disappointment – that day I had no money with me. However, the trusting manager said, 'No problem – here is the "Combined". Bring the money in tomorrow.'

I was overjoyed as I had never had one before – I just had the 2s 6d Eastern Region and Midland Region books. Thanks for trusting me, Mr Smiths Manager! My collection of 'tools of the trade' for spotting was now complete, others items being the *Locoshed Book*, giving you the home shed of every engine, *The British*

Locomotive Shed Directory, which was invaluable for giving directions from the main station to each shed, *Trains Illustrated* magazine, for articles and monthly updates regarding locomotive transfers and withdrawals, and a notebook for my own records.

In the summer of 1960 four of us started to go for a day's spotting at Ranskill – on the Eastern Region main line – on Thursdays, the 9 miles taking about half an hour on our bikes. For our day's food we would take with us eggs, a tin of beans with sausages, and lard, cooking them on a small methylated spirits camping stove using a frying pan we had bought from the local Army & Navy Stores. Looking back on it now, obviously none of our parents had any conception of the possible dangers to which 12-year-old children were exposed with matches and methylated spirits, but we enjoyed it and survived. Late afternoon I would pack up my things, washing the frying pan with clods of grass and earth, and head for home at about 5.30 so I could be there when the pub opened at 6 to sell sweets in the off-licence. My spotting mates would stay on for another couple of hours – there was no hint of the Three Musketeers spirit ('united we stand, divided we fall' or 'all for one and one for all'),

but nevertheless we would meet up again at about 7.30 at the fish and chip shop for an update on what I had missed.

One of these lineside spotting trips gave me one of my many memorable moments in life to treasure – you know the ones, they are vividly recalled to your memory and you can nearly touch the images. The reason we used to go to Ranskill on a Thursday was because spotters knew it locally as trial day, when locomotives would be outshopped from Doncaster Plant at about midday on the 'Plant stream'; this was about six engines coupled together that left the Plant and passed through the station area and into the shed. Some of them had only gone in for light repair, but those that had been given a general had also been immaculately repainted, and they were the ones that later in the afternoon would been sent out light engine for a trial run down to Grantham, turning on the triangle and returning to Doncaster shed. Well, this was mid-afternoon on Thursday 28 July 1960 and ex-works Class 'A3' No 60100 *Spearmint* passed through light from Doncaster. It was a 'cop' for me, as she was a Scottish-based 'A3' that was not a regular visitor south of York – but that was not the image that stuck with me. It was her return trip to Doncaster, passing us at about 5 o'clock. The sun was lower and as *Spearmint* passed it seemed to reflect more than ever off the freshly painted casing – it was pristine. But what was everlasting for me was the near silence as it passed, other than the shhhh … shhhh … shhhh … shhhh sound of steam being emitted from the cylinder cocks at the bottom of the cylinders. The movement was effortless, and I can see and hear it as I write this.

Another vivid memory was when I went on holiday to Blackpool with my Dad, as we did every year – Mam had to stay at home and look after the pub. Going by train, we passed Preston shed which just contained 11 un-rebuilt 'Patriots' in store. I didn't manage to get all the numbers, so during the holiday, when I went

spotting one day at Blackpool Central, I caught a train to Preston, intending to go round the shed. But no such luck – the foreman would not let me round, and when I asked him for a list of what was on shed it was 'Get out now!' It took me a good few years to actually track down what the 'Patriots' were, but I managed it, initially aided by the postcard sent to me from Blackpool by my spotting friend Stuart Taylor. Unfortunately those early days are just memories, as I did not own a camera at that time.

When I started taking photos my friend Alan Smalley told me that it was impossible to combine spotting with taking pictures it was either one or the other. I was very impressionable at that time, particularly as Alan was about five years my senior; I hung on to his every word, as he was very knowledgeable about railways and even more so about photography. So I gave it a go, stopped spotting and just took photos. We went on two trips within a week, first to Skipton then to Basingstoke. It was good, but I really missed the thrill of spotting, so I quickly went back to both! Alan did wedding photography as a sideline and owned a Contarex, a Pentax and two Roliflexes; he also did all his own developing and printing to a very high standard. Over a 12-month period he gave me a good insight into all aspects of photography, but our friendship slowly waned because he had a girlfriend and it became obvious that they did not want me tagging along every night, so I went my own way, but to Alan – my photography mentor – I will always be eternally grateful.

At the age of 14 I was allowed to travel

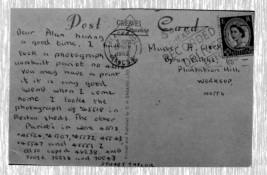

anywhere on my own with my parents' approval, so my jaunts took me the length and breadth of the country. Unfortunately my Dad died when I was just 15, so I was given more jobs to do at the pub, like opening up at 6 o'clock on Monday to Friday and serving until 7 o'clock, when the part-time bar staff would start, then I would rush down and meet my mates at the fish and chip shop for a couple of hours in the evening. The only likelihood of a cop was whatever was on the fish train at about 7 o'clock, which could be anything from a '9F', a 'V2', a 'K3' or a 'B1'. I'm not sure where it came from, but it was likely either Grimsby or Hull.

In 1963, having no serious thoughts about a career and in the absence of any guidance from my parents, I decided to leave school at the earliest opportunity when I was 15. I had no intention of further education, and university was not even a consideration– as far as I was concerned that was something for the 'well-off' to do. I had an interview with the schools careers officer, who asked me what I had in mind for my working life, and my reply to him was that I wanted to work in an office. He must have thought 'dickhead' – no ambition. Anyway, he obviously took my words on board because about three weeks later he told me that a local family-run company, Oats Ltd, which manufactured wooden tool handles, wanted a junior to work in the production office under the supervision of one of the senior family member's sons. I was delighted and an interview was arranged for the next morning. I was told that if I was successful I could leave school immediately and not wait until the end of the summer term, as my birth date allowed this.

Obviously I was a bit 'green', having no interview skills, and Edward de Bono's Lateral Thinking Techniques didn't arrive on the scene until the late 1960s, but I think I did pretty well as I was offered the job at the interview, starting at £3 2s 6d for a five-day week with two weeks holiday a year. I said I could start on Monday, thank you very much!

That was perfect as my mother had already told me that as long as I continued to cover the first hour in the pub on Monday to Friday she would not take any payment for board and lodging from me, so that meant all the pay was mine. Great!

Working in a factory office and having to walk through the factory on a regular basis really exposed me to the usual pranks from the older employees, but I did not let it get to me – I just laughed and took it in good spirit. I think that when people realised they were not upsetting me the pranks tailed off. Having said that, though, I never told anyone at work that I was a trainspotter, because I knew that would be ammunition for some real ridicule. I remember going on a works trip to London for a weekend. My intention was shed visits, while everybody else's was beer, clubs and Soho. Both mornings I would get up very early at the guest house, before anyone else, have my breakfast and was gone before the others woke up, saving me from having to make any excuse not to go with them for the day.

I did most of the London sheds over that weekend, but when asked where I had been I said, 'Just the usual sightseeing,' and got away with it.

I progressed from doing sheds on my own and with mates to going on organised trips by coach, doing anything between 6 and 12 sheds in one area. There were many clubs that promoted this, advertising in my monthly bible, *Trains Illustrated*, but the ones I joined up with were the Derbyshire Railway Society, the Warwickshire Railway Society and Scottish Railfans.

They did not pick up from the Worksop area, so I had to make my own way to the pick-up place, which was either Derby, Birmingham or Carlisle respectively. No problem – it just meant that I usually had to catch a train the night before or very early on the day of the trip. Included here is a photo of my trainspotting partner-in-crime John Charnock, clutching his notebook and pen and doing his Marty Feldman impression just as we entered Derby, where we would meet the rest of the Derbyshire Railway Society members for a coach visit to Bristol and South Wales.

Visits were always at a weekend, either on Saturday or Sunday or both; Sunday visits were always the best as depots would be full. The longest shed bash I did was with the Warwickshire Railway Society, visiting 67 sheds in the North East, North West, North Yorkshire, Carlisle, and the Glasgow and Edinburgh area, spotting 2,364 locos and copping 1,482, a very good percentage.

Our base was at Hest Bank in the camping coaches by the station, and the price was ridiculously cheap at £12 1s 6d; this included the camping coach for six nights, a guesthouse stay for one night in Scotland, coach and rail travel for the week, and your return fare from home to Hest Bank. How they managed to promote it at that bargain price I don't know, but well done the Warwickshire Railway Society!

It is a wonder we survived, because the only food provided was breakfast on the one morning we were at the guesthouse, and I can only recall stocking up on drink and Lyons individual fruit pies once at Middlesbrough. I really cannot recall eating much at all. I certainly lived and died in the same clothes! I know I took two polyester drip-dry shirts – they were very fashionable then – your underpants were the ones you had on, and having a wash was every other day when you returned to the camping coach, but it was great. At the end of the week we drew lots for who was going to empty what looked like a large oil drum that contained all the toilet waste. Luckily it wasn't me! I got home on the Saturday at about 4 o'clock in the afternoon, then after a bath and a quick 'Hello, and how was your week?' from Mam it was down to the lineside by the chip shop with my spotting mates at the usual time of 7.

The only down side to the organised trips was that they started visits very early in the morning when it was dark, and if it was a two-day trip you would be going around sheds in the dark and at night, so torches were a necessity, but photographs were impossible. Also, if you were visiting during the night you could be asleep on the coach and no one would wake you up – they just left you on your seat. I remember on a 'two-dayer' to South Wales I missed Aberdare and Aberbeeg because I was asleep – it's too late when it's happened.

I would like to record that a review of my first book appeared in one of the monthly railway magazines and was read by my long-lost friend John Charnock ('Channy'), and as a result we managed to get in touch again after 50-odd years, so all the work in respect of the preparation of that book was well worth it just to re-establish that friendship. Well, this my second book and continues with the same format as the first, black and white photographs and text about the subject locomotive together with, where appropriate, general information regarding events of the day, making it in some instances a somewhat light-hearted account. Here's hoping you enjoy this latest selection from my treasured library of photographs!

1 • Trip to Carlisle

Carlisle, the only city in Cumbria, is situated between the Scottish border to the north and the Lake District to the south, with the western extremity of Hadrian's Wall passing through. Industry was largely textile mills and engineering works, but at the start of the 20th century the textile industry was in decline due to technological advancements in machinery, making the once labour-intensive industry more automated, and the inevitable redundancies followed. However, probably the most recognisable employer now is Eddie Stobart Ltd, the haulage company with trucks that are all named after females, which has its own army of enthusiasts spotting the truck names, now amounting to in excess of 2,500 in the fleet. The company, whose headquarters is still in Carlisle, has diversified into railway infrastructure and engineering, Carlisle Lake District Airport, and in 2008 it purchased London Southend Airport.

Railways have of course always been a part of the history of Carlisle. In the early days there were seven railway companies using Citadel station, now a Grade II-listed building, and I would think that is due mainly to the magnificent neo-Tudor frontage. Peripheral to the station there were three locomotive sheds: Kingmoor at the northern end, which at one time incorporated the largest railway marshalling yard in Europe; Upperby at the south end; and Canal to the west. Upperby and Canal have long gone, but Kingmoor, albeit rebuilt as a Traction Maintenance Depot, still exists, but on the opposite side of the West Coast Main Line from the original steam shed.

Having entered service one month earlier to the accompaniment of the Beatles and *Please Please Me*, English Electric Type 3 No D6818 is at Sheffield Victoria, with maybe a train for Lincoln. A Derby-built diesel multiple unit is parked in the middle road, one of a set of 50 that at this time were all stabled at Sheffield Darnall and Lincoln, performing duties between the two cities and associated routes for 25 years. (April 1963)

Left: Workhorses for the area were the 'B1s', with allocations to Darnall, Canklow, Doncaster and Retford. No 61051, off Canklow, makes a spirited light engine start at Sheffield Midland pulling away from the rake of coaches that she's left in one of the middle roads after doing a bit of shunting work. Eventually her sister engine No 61050 would take them away. (13 June 1963)

Below: Parked in bay Platform 7 underneath the footbridge that leads to Norfolk Park, 1946 Ivatt Class 2MT No 46401 'blows off' before pulling away. Although she looks interested, the woman can't possibly still be thinking of climbing aboard! (13 June 1963)

Below: Two sets of double-headed 'Peaks': the second of each pair is unidentified, but the leaders are No D84 on the right and No D36 on the left, posing at the North Junction signal box and heading north, probably double-headed at Chesterfield to assist climbing the gradients. Note the two styles of loco headcode panels, centre and split. (1960)

Above: Here we have one of the replacements for the 'Jubilee' and 'Royal Scot' classes in the form of Sulzer Type 4 'Peak' No D34 with a train from the south entering Midland station, and another Peak ready to leave next to the high, imposing buttressed retaining walls that were a distinctive feature of that end of the station. In the carriage and goods sidings to the right is a diesel shunter and the nose of York-based 'V2' No 60855. (13 June 1963)

Left: Another double-header, but this time it is an unidentified 'Black Five' – it was not a case of locomotive failure as the Stanier is taking on water for the rest of the journey – being assisted by Sulzer Type 4 No D103, with one of her crew climbing down from the cab to carry out some inspection of the diesel before heading north with the express. (1960)

Right: Starting out from Leeds City heading the inter-regional service 'The Devonian' and carrying a BR Type 3-style headboard with a red background is 'Jubilee' Class No 45605 *Cyprus*. The 'Jubilee' would be in charge until Bristol, then a Western Region engine would take control to Paignton; the headboard would have to be changed to a Western-style one as the lamp brackets differed from the LMS locos. Just above the tender you can see the LMS's Queens Hotel, which is still there mostly unchanged today, but Leeds City station has been revamped twice since this image.

1960 was a significant date for Cyprus, as it gained independence from the UK on 16 August, but it was the start of 40 years of conflict between the Greek and Turkish Cypriots, which has really only just got to the toleration state between them both – it does take generations to finally accept an agreement in any conflict. (1960)

Below: Peppercorn Class 'A1' 'Pacific' No 60134 *Foxhunter* stands at the western end of 55H Neville Hill in reasonable condition; it lasted for just over another year, then was sold for scrap to T. W. Ward at Beighton in November 1965. Throughout her 17 years of service she had six Diagram 118 boilers fitted, the last in October 1962. (29 July 1964)

Abovet: Inside one of the two roundhouses at Neville Hill, which had been reroofed in 1958, making them unusually bright for a steam shed, is another of the depot's own Class 'A1s', No 60154 *Bon Accord*, in top-class condition – you can almost see the Brunswick Green. Over her 16 years of service she had eight Diagram 118 boilers – that's one every two years, which seems an awful lot to me!

At this time in her namesake's town of Aberdeen the medical situation was at a serious level with 398 confirmed and 52 suspected cases of typhoid, which were eventually traced to tinned corned beef from South America. According to Hansard (HC Deb 29 July 1964 vol 699 cc1411-3) Mr Jo Grimond noticed that certain types of pressed beef had disappeared from the Tea Room in the House of Commons, forcing him to question the Secretary of State for Scotland as to whether there had been a general withdrawal. The answer from Mr Noble was 'No'. (29 July 1964)

Under wraps is Class 'K4' *The Great Marquess*, formerly BR No 61994 but now repainted in Apple Green back to LNER days as No 3442. She was owned by Viscount Garnock, who had an arrangement for her to be stabled at Neville Hill when not being employed on special trains. This lasted until the 1968 BR ban on steam workings. The current owner, John Cameron, has decided not to invest any more money to get another running certificate after much good service on the West Highland Line, and she will now soon be part of his static display in a new farming and railway visitor centre at his farm in St Monans, Fife – but a big thank you to John, because without such enthusiasts and investors the world would be a smaller place! (29 July 1964)

Having just entered 55A Holbeck, I am spotted by a young fireman (perhaps), who is really no threat to me, my biggest challenge being to avoid the glances of the shed foremen in the long blue smock standing at the corner of the office on the right but looking in the opposite direction. I wasn't spotted that day, but I did spot a good few locos on shed, the first being the 'Black Five' in front of me, No 44727. (1960)

Apart from the double chimney, which was fitted in August 1959, Class 'A3' No 60038 *Firdaussi* is seen virtually as built (1934) at Holbeck shed. Always based in the north, she was relocated between Gateshead, Heaton, Darlington and Leeds during her 29 years of service.

Tottenham Hotspur were embarking on their epic double winning season and were undefeated in the first 16 games until they came up against Sheffield Wednesday and lost 2-1. I can remember that every Saturday on the black and white television news broadcasts they only showed highlights from one match, and it was always Spurs, and if you missed the goals there were no reruns – you'd had it. (1960)

Below: Not the footballers' injury but the Greek hero of the Trojan War, this is *Achilles*, 'Jubilee' Class locomotive No 45697, already coaled and now taking on water, the two elements required by a steam loco. Standing just in front of the coaling tower at Leeds Holbeck, she will soon be 'ready for the off'. (29 July 1964)

Above: With the Yorkshire Dales in the background, here is a general view of Skipton station with an unidentified Peak, and a DMU set waiting for a departure south. On the right are the slightly elevated Platforms 5 and 6 serving Ilkley; both used to have canopies along their entire length but they were removed in LMS days, although the canopy stanchions are still visible and intact. You can almost hear the haunting sound of Kyu Sakamoto singing *Sukiyaki* echoing from the hills – it was being played hourly on the radio in the UK and reached No 1 in the US. In the UK it was also covered instrumentally by Kenny Ball and his Jazzmen, reaching No 10 in the charts. (13 June 1963)

Below: 'Coronation' Class No 46238 *City of Carlisle,* in what you could describe as pristine condition, is on a freight duty, which was not in Stanier's thoughts back in 1937 when they were introduced on the LMS. *City of Carlisle* was originally built with a streamlined casing, together with 23 other members of the class. A lone brake-van is on the other middle road next to a 'Peak' double-heading with a 'Black Five' on a passenger train. This was actually my first glimpse of Carlisle Citadel station, and what a lasting memory – it really is impossible to recreate scenes like this, although pre-arranged photo shoots do their best. (30 November 1963)

Above: The Hughes/Fowler 'Crabs' were introduced in 1926, and this example, No 42819, entered service in 1929 and is standing by the coal stage that was just east of the main shed at 24G Skipton. (29 July 1964)

Above: According to the *Shed Directory*, the walking time to Carlisle Canal was 35 minutes, and I just had to make an early morning visit although I knew the shed had officially closed on 10 June 1963. I just thought that there might be the slightest chance that my elusive remaining Class 'A3s' might still be there, but it wasn't to be – completely empty! (30 November 1963)

Right: So another walk, this time of 45 minutes, brought me to 12A Kingmoor, where the allocation was about 140. This was midweek, a Thursday, but we were glad to see 107 on shed. This is the view from the southern end of the shed with a predominance of steam, albeit that a few were dead. (30 July 1964)

Above: If any class of locomotive visually displayed elegance and power, then for lots of spotters this was it! In maroon livery (red to us youngsters), which at the time no other region employed, is 'Coronation' Class No 46244 *King George VI*. The driver, with his hand on the regulator, possibly singing the P. J. Proby hit *Hold Me*, is getting ready to ease out of Kingmoor for his next duty. (30 July 1964)

Above right: Having entered service in 1929, Fowler Class 4 2-6-4 tank No 42353, with parallel boiler, is amongst the stored line at Kingmoor. Her fate had been officially confirmed a month earlier in June, and she was broken up at Arnott Young of Carmyle, which started scrapping locomotives in 1960, the last example being in 1968. (30 July 1964)

Right: 'Royal Scot' Class No 46132 *The King's Regiment Liverpool* had been transferred from Upperby to Kingmoor, but was surplus to requirements and was withdrawn on 1 February 1964 and sold for scrap to Arnott Young at Troon. (30 July 1964)

Right: The Carlisle sheds did have a predominance of LMS locomotives, but visitors from the former LNER were frequent, although not in great numbers. Visiting today is Class 'V2' No 60970 off 64A St Margarets, in steam having probably brought a freight down from Scotland to be sorted in the Kingmoor yards. Having said that, most steam locos were then on freight duties. (30 July 1964)

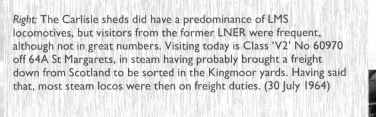

Left: 'Clan' Class No 72009 *Clan Stewart* was always a Kingmoor locomotive except for a one-month spell in 1958 when she was transferred to Stratford for trials – obviously the crews did not get on with her, so back to Kingmoor she came. As with all of them, the driver was quite happy to pose for me – it's a great pity I didn't take their names. (30 July 1964)

At the northern end of Kingmoor is a new arrival, having relocated from Willesden in September. Rebuilt 'Patriot' No 45527 *Southport* was one of 13 of the class to sport names of holiday resorts of the North West and North Wales. (30 July 1964)

Above: Still in Kingmoor, this is 'Jubilee' Class No 45696 *Arethusa*, a Greek mythological character whose name meant 'the waterer', but it did not exclude her from going to the water tower – she had no privileges! She is coupled to one of the smaller versions of Fowler tender, which is really filled to the limit – good job it has the side rails! (30 July 1964)

Right and above right: Entering Upperby by the locally known entrance nicknamed 'Burma Road', we saw stored 'Patriot' No 45545 *Planet*. If you have a copy of Julian Holland's great book *The Lost Joy of Railways* and go to page 137, you will see an almost identical photo and notebook entries, as Julian's visit was the day before mine. There are even similarities in our childlike handwriting styles! (30 July 1964)

Above: 'Coronation' Class No 46226 *Duchess of Norfolk* stands at the buffers in front of the southern end of Upperby's concrete roundhouse with sacking over the chimney, waiting in hope! (30 November 1963)

Above right: Inside Upperby's roundhouse is green-liveried 'Coronation' Class No 46255 *City of Hereford*, glistening with the aid of light coming in from the roof but mainly from the side windows of this relatively newly constructed (1948) 32-road roundhouse with its 70-foot turntable. (30 November 1963)

Right: Always based on the LMS main line, being previously shedded at Camden and Crewe, 'Coronation' Class No 46225 *Duchess of Gloucester* is at her final home of Upperby in steam and still reasonably employed, but will be withdrawn in October and cut up by the end of the year at Arnott Young of Troon. (30 July 1964)

Built in 1933, Stanier-design 'Princess' Class No 46200 *The Princess Royal* was not so lucky, being withdrawn in November 1962 and stored at both Kingmoor and Upperby for two years with connecting rods removed but still elegant. She is seen here at her final location in Upperby just in front of the stores shed, having previously been dumped in the sidings near 'Burma Road'. (30 July 1964)

Left: There did seem to be plenty of 'Coronations' about at Upperby and in service, but this one, No 46228 *Duchess of Rutland*, was in a very unkempt condition; maybe they knew she was to be withdrawn in October so didn't bother. I had seen her four days before on Polmadie, so she was getting a bit of employment. (30 July 1964)

After coming off the freight seen in the earlier photo (page 18),
the pride of Carlisle Upperby, 'Coronation' Class No 46238 *City
of Carlisle*, is in resplendent condition. (30 November 1963)

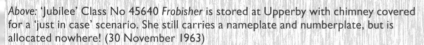

Above: 'Jubilee' Class No 45640 *Frobisher* is stored at Upperby with chimney covered for a 'just in case' scenario. She still carries a nameplate and numberplate, but is allocated nowhere! (30 November 1963)

Above right: You would think that Ivatt Class 2 2-6-0 No 46458 had very recently had a service in the works, as it is in almost ex-works condition, but you never know. Upperby did a have a good reputation for clean locos, so had the cleaners concentrated their efforts on this Class 2? (30 November 1963)

Right: Similar front ends but different classes: on the left is 'Royal Scot' Class No 46128 *The Lovat Scouts* and on the right 'Patriot' Class No 45535 *Sir Herbert Walker K.C.B.*, which was moved from Upperby to Annesley on 29 January 1964 for a further six months in storage – obviously none of the local scrap merchants had put in an acceptable bid. (30 November 1963)

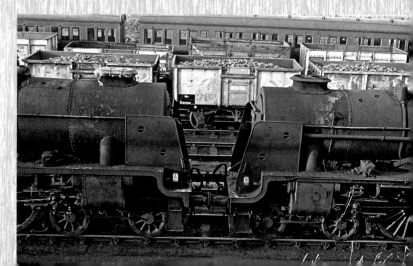

This is the 'Royal Scot' in full view. No 46128 *The Lovat Scouts* is devoid of nameplates, and I don't think she moved from this position until officially condemned in May 1965. Behind her are two rows of coal wagons, one full, the other empty, and a row of non-corridor carriages; if my memory serves me right these were from the Scottish Region, but I'm open to correction… (30 November 1963)

2 • Gloucester and Bristol

Gloucester and Bristol have many similarities: both are situated along the banks of the River Severn/Bristol Channel, and each had its own port. The River Port of Gloucester accessed the River Severn by means of the Gloucester & Sharpness Canal; the port is now closed to cargo vessels and is a waterfront area. Bristol's original docks have also closed and were moved to Avonmouth and the recently constructed Royal Portbury Docks. The original city dock is now also a waterfront attraction and is the permanent home of Isambard Kingdom Brunel's SS *Great Britain*.

Both cities also have an aviation and aerospace background. Gloucester had the Gloster Aircraft Company based in the suburb of Brockworth and was heavily involved with Frank Whittle and the development of the turbojet engine. The first British jet aircraft, the experimental Gloster E.28/39, took off from the company's airfield and prompted the development of the Gloster Meteor, the only jet to be used by the Allied forces in the Second World War.

Bristol's claim to fame was its involvement with the development of the Anglo-French Concorde in the 1960s. The British aircraft, under the captaincy of Brian Trubshaw, made its maiden flight on 9 April 1969 from the Bristol Aeroplane Company at Filton.

In respect of railways, both cities were important and both were served by the Great Western and the London Midland & Scottish. Gloucester had two engine sheds at Horton Road and Barnwood, and Bristol had three, at Bath Road, St Phillips Marsh and Barrow Road. All are now closed except St Phillips Marsh TMD, which is primarily used for the maintenance of the InterCity 125 trains.

Beyer Peacock 'Hymek' Type 3 No D7017 is pulling away from Gloucester station and passing Horton Road depot on the right and Gloucester Cathedral in view just above the coaches. The train indicator panel suggests that it is destined for the London Midland Region, likely going to Birmingham or beyond. (11 July 1964)

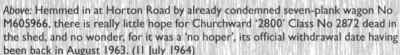

Above: Hemmed in at Horton Road by already condemned seven-plank wagon No M605966, there is really little hope for Churchward '2800' Class No 2872 dead in the shed, and no wonder, for it was a 'no hoper', its official withdrawal date having been back in August 1963. (11 July 1964)

Above right: 'Modified Hall' No 6995 *Benthall Hall* still going, and is seen standing on the approaches to Horton Road. She was eventually withdrawn in March 1965 and scrapped in July at Birds of Risca, South Wales. The gasometer on the left lasted longer, being scrapped in situ during October 2012. (11 July 1964)

Right: 'Hall' Class No 6947 *Helmingham Hall* stands idle in Horton Road, with the forthcoming World Cup of 1966 being advertised on the Shell oil wagon! Little could they have imagined what the outcome would be! No 6947 was broken up at Cashmore's of Newport three months before the competition, so when you hear, 'They think it's all over – it is now,' they certainly weren't talking about her, as it was already over... (11 July 1964)

BR Standard Class 5MT No 73093 was not withdrawn until July 1967, so still had plenty of steaming left in her. She is seen here resting at Horton Road, but would be transferred to Bath, then Guildford, before she was cut up at Cashmore's of Newport, probably forming part of the famous 40-foot pile of scrap boilers, etc, that was visible from the newly constructed George Street Bridge in Newport. (11 July 1964)

On home territory at Horton Road is Class '5101' 2-6-2 tank No 4104, standing next to the coaling stage and a couple of BR Standard Class 9Fs, looking very smart and a credit to the shed cleaners – although it could have been the result of activity by the unofficial cleaning group of spotters making her presentable for the scrapyard, because according to records her fate had already been announced in May and she was moved to Cashmore's of Newport later in July for cutting up. (11 July 1964)

Left: Over at 82E Barrow Road, Bristol's LMS shed, four spotters have possibly climbed over at Days Bridge and are now thinking about their next move from just in front of the dead row, with 4F 0-6-0 No 44296 first in line. (11 July 1964)

Above: '5700' Class pannier tank No 4684 is further along the dead row. After having been allocated in Wales since birth in 1944, she moved to Barrow Road for the last two years, only working for about one of them. She will now move no more, until towed back to Wales, to Cashmore's of Newport, for the inevitable. (11 July 1964)

Right: There are close on 30 locomotives in this general view of stored and active Western and London Midland locos and BR Standards in the sidings adjacent to the roundhouse on the left. The Barrow Road overbridge is on the horizon and the main Bristol to Gloucester line is on the right; the inspection pits beneath these four roads could obviously not be used to their full advantage. (11 July 1964)

Inside the 24-road roundhouse at Barrow Road with its 60-foot turntable are 'Jubilee' Class No 45682 *Trafalgar*, quietly steaming and preparing for battle, and sister loco No 45626 *Seychelles*, tranquil like the archipelago. (11 July 1964)

Above: Designed at Doncaster, but this example built at Derby and now 14 years old, is British Railways Standard Class 5MT No 73015, standing at the front of Barrow Road shed on the inspection pit near the carriage sidings. (11 July 1964)

Above right: 'Black Five' No 44843 has presumably just come off train 2Z99. In front is a spotter, hands on head, trying to decide which of the four rows to do first. The nice undamaged brass cabside plate of No 9601 is also in view. (11 July 1964)

Right: Still with plenty of work available for the survivors, here we have ex-LMS 8F No 48460 simmering and at the ready. (11 July 1964)

The lyrics of the just released Beatles track and film *A Hard Day's Night* – 'I've been working like a dog' – sum up the thoughts of 9F 2-10-0s Nos 92128 and 92151, both in an almost identical state having come off Saltley with freight workings from the Midlands and now resting in the live roads of Barrow Road. (11 July 1964)

Diminutive Class '5700' pannier tank No 4626 is dwarfed by a skyline dominated by one of the two gasometers at the side of the depot. Entering service in 1942 and allocated to Cardiff East Dock, Abercynon, Dover, Salisbury and now resting at Barrow Road, she has an affinity with the Beach Boys and their then current hit, *I Get Around*. (11 July 1964)

A fine example of a 'Jubilee' Class 4-6-0 is No 45674 *Duncan* from 2E Saltley, most likely having worked a passenger train down from Birmingham earlier and now waiting for the next published roster, hoping for a return home. (11 July 1964)

Class '5700' No 9601, with an unusual style of smokebox numberplate but with the traditional brass cabside of the Great Western on the bunker, stands at the extreme end of the dead lines and may not be moving again until the official withdrawal notice is served in December. (11 July 1964)

This general view of 82A Bristol Bath Road features five 'Western' Class and two 'Hymek' diesel-hydraulics standing in the open yard in front of the curves of the station in the background. The cleanliness of the approaches to the depot is very noticeable in comparison to the grimy steam sheds, full of waste ash. (11 July 1964)

Above: Brush Type 4 No D1724 looks brand new with one of the maintenance crew shining up the front beam and the other two doing nothing, with hands behind their backs. According to M. Farouk Radian MSc, an expert in body language, hands behind the back signifies a person who is confident and on top of matters in a current situation, so everything seems fine – Hakuna Matata! (11 July 1964)

Left: At 11.23am we are in the depot with an assortment of main-line diesels: 'Warship' No D819 *Goliath*, 'Western' No D1043 *Western Duke*, Sulzer Type 4 No D41, Brush Type 4 No D1722, and another Sulzer Type 4, No D190. I may have spoken too soon about cleanliness, looking at the two piles in the foreground, but it's not spent ash, just building material, sand and chippings presumably for the work going on around the depot. (11 July 1964)

Below: North British Type 2 No D6355 stands in the centre of a clutch of 'Hymek', Nos D7066, D7027 and the smoky one unidentified. (11 July 1964)

Above: 'Western' Class No D1065 *Western Consort* is in the company of D1002 *Western Explorer* on the left and D1072 *Western Glory* in the background; considering that *Consort* entered service the previous summer, her condition is 'as new'. The shed foreman looks smart as well, chaperoning our party around the depot and anxiously stopping and looking behind for stragglers with safety in mind. (11 July 1964)

Percy Main is on the 55th parallel north and on the northern banks of the River Tyne. It was originally a pit village, the mine being known both as Percy Main Colliery and Howden Panns Colliery. Coal was excavated between the shaft depths of 700 feet (High Main Seam) and 950 feet (Bensham Seam).

Over a period of 250 years there were more than 100 collieries and pits within 5 miles of Percy Main, so it goes without saying that the main employer in the area was mining, together with associated industries.

Percy Main and the surrounding area is now part of the modern district of North Tyneside and is on the Yellow line of the Tyne & Wear Metro. The mines have gone and been replaced by many housing estates.

It is no wonder that the 'J27' Class 0-6-0s dominated the tracks around Percy

Just after midnight at a cold and draughty platform at York, 9F No 92201 pauses for loading on a mixed parcels duty, while on the other side of the world Ngo Dinh Diem of South Vietnam had just been overthrown in a successful coup d'état, I was obviously better off out of it at York! (2 November 1963)

Main, having proved their capability to work on the short trips transporting coal from the mines to the shipping staithes along the Tyne.

The locomotive shed at Percy Main was about a 10-minute walk from the station, whose footbridge, installed by the North Eastern Railway, has been preserved by the National Railway Museum in York. The shed had a run-down appearance and some buildings were roofless, but it was apparent that the stock of locomotives were little workhorses – they were always steamed, dirty, ready and working, as proven by the following photographs.

Above: English Electric Type 4 No D286 is being loaded up at York with mail and parcels, one of the night-time routines that were very predictable and had prompted the 'Great Train Robbery' earlier in the year. (2 November 1963)

Left: An unidentified Brush Type 4 stands in Platform 9, protected from the elements by the great arches of York, awaiting the 'off' to the north. (2 November 1963)

Left: Taken from the southern end of the platforms at Newcastle Central, English Electric Type 4 No D378 is on a southbound freight taking the left-hand curve that will take it over the King Edward Bridge and past Gateshead depot, which will be on the left but unfortunately with limited viewing from a carriage for spotters. (2 November 1963)

Below: Approaching in the opposite direction is English Electric Type 4 No D385 on a mixed freight heading north and taking the freight avoiding line. (2 November 1963)

Below: This is what I had come to see before the proposed end of steam duties at Percy Main. In a couple of weeks English Electric Type 3s would be taking over the work responsibilities of the 'J27s', and here No 65802 negotiates what will soon become completely overgrown tracks – it doesn't appear to be far off that now! (2 November 1963)

Above: In this view from the main line at Percy Main, Class 'J27' No 65814 is having a rest in the roofless three-road through shed together with a few others of the class. There were two more shed buildings behind this one, a stone-built two-road shed and a brick-built three-road shed, both dead-ended. All is peaceful – who would have thought that 20 days later the world would be in turmoil with the news of the assassination of John F. Kennedy, one of life's 'Where were you when…?' (2 November 1963)

No 65861 is on a short journey, but making absolutely sure she can stop by having five brake-vans coupled! (2 November 1963)

It was thought to be the last few days of steam at Percy Main, and No 65817 is being driven by an obviously enthusiastic and patriotic crew; however, assuming the flagpole was to be on the left, the Union Jack is the wrong way up (the flag is not reflective symmetrically) – but it's the thought that counts. Having said that, it is still theoretically a crime to fly the flag incorrectly in the UK and the Commonwealth, termed as 'lese-majesty', meaning insulting the Crown. (2 November 1963)

No 65795 makes a spirited departure from the coaling stage area, but I'm not sure if the wagons were fully loaded or were just being shunted around empty. Nevertheless it was an atmospheric moment by a member the class. (2 November 1963)

No 65813 is taking on water, probably doing so many times during the shift, posing next to the water storage facility on the right and just in front on the roofed shed buildings; the turntable is partially visible to the left of the tender. (2 November 1963)

Above: Percy Main's allocation was all 'J27s', which were employed daily on moving coal from the Northumberland mines to the wooden coal staithes along the Tyne, mainly at Dunston, Blyth and North Shields, from where it was loaded onto ships for distribution all over the UK. Here you see No 65817 with a load of empties going back for a refill. The coal staithes of Blyth were featured in the 1971 film *Get Carter,* starring Michael Caine. (2 November 1963)

Above: My photographic mentor Alan Smalley, in a warm coat with camera case, flat cap and his Contarex, takes a picture of 'J27' No 65817 from a different angle, obviously thinking it would be a better composition than mine – but was it? (2 November 1963)

Right: No 65817 is seen again taking the empty mineral wagons under the road overbridge leading towards the coaling stage, the ramped approach of which can be clearly seen. (2 November 1963)

Pausing at the signal gantry opposite the sheds with her canvas 'weather' canopy partially drawn down, No 65817 is now running tender-first; there was no real need to turn the locos on these duties. Another working is disappearing under the road overbridge, going in the opposite direction. (2 November 1963)

No 65817 is on the curve and just passing the ramped coaling stage that, according to reports, was not the ideal location for the facility, being a long way from the sheds, and locos would have to negotiate a few points along the main line to get to it. (2 November 1963)

Below: No 65814 has moved up a bit and is inching forward around the curve. Can I hear Roy Orbison in the distance singing *It's Over*? It was No 1 in the charts at the beginning of the month, but it was still not over for the 'J27' 0-6-0s at Percy Main. (27 July 1964)

Above: Some six months later at Percy Main on a fine summer's day, contrary to what had been proposed there were still some steam duties left, and No 65814 waits for the signal to move off. Everything is looking neat, clean and tidy – the crews seemed to take a pride in their engines and work. (27 July 1964)

4 • Trip to Shrewsbury

Shrewsbury is a market town situated 9 miles east of the Welsh border and noted for the annual mid-August Flower Show, one of the largest horticultural shows in England, attracting around 60,000 visitors each day and accredited by the *Guinness Book of Records* as the longest-running flower show in the world.

Although now in England, Shrewsbury was once the early capital of the Kingdom of Powys in Wales, and over the subsequent years in medieval times was at the forefront of many a battle between the two countries for control and ownership.

Charles Darwin was born in Shrewsbury in 1809 and spent his early life there before writing *On the Origin of Species*, which was published in 1859 to mixed reviews, particularly from the Church, but over the years his theories have proved to be realistic and it has been voted the most influential academic book ever written.

In a totally different sphere, Arthur Rowley, who latterly played for Shrewsbury Town FC, holds the record for the most goals scored – 433 (not all for Shrewsbury) over a 19-year period – a record that will probably never to be beaten. His last game was in 1965.

Alexander Walter Barr 'Sandy' Lyle, the professional golfer, was born in Shrewsbury in 1958, but for reasons I cannot understand decided to represent Scotland throughout his career. He was also a member of five Ryder Cup teams, probably the most notable victory being that in 1987, for the first time ever on American soil.

Having covered the Worksop to Crewe route in my the first book, I will take up the journey to Shrewsbury at Crewe, where 'Patriot' Class No 45526 *Morecambe and Heysham* departs with an express to Glasgow. The sight of steam on main-line expresses was becoming rarer by the day, and I now feel privileged to have witnessed and captured this one. (27 July 1963)

Immediately after leaving Crewe southbound we take the right-hand curve onto the Shrewsbury line and pass BR Standard Class 4MT No 75003 waiting to couple up to the coaches that are out of view and head back to the Machynlleth area, which was her home shed. (30 July 1963)

Above: A little further on BR Standard Class 2MT No 78030 is on empty stock duties, stationary and parked virtually on the bridge over the freight avoiding line, the catenary of which is just visible on the left; the line was constructed between 1896 and 1901 and skirted the station on the west side, rejoining it beyond the North and South junctions. (30 July 1963)

Right: 'Grange' Class No 6851 *Hurst Grange*, on a northbound freight from the Shrewsbury area, passes the freight yards south-west of Crewe. As you can see, by now even the freight yard had been fully electrified. (30 July 1963)

Left: British Railways' equivalent to the 1959 play and film *The Long and the Short and the Tall* is these two semaphores, and between them a train hauled by 'Manor' No 7801 *Anthony Manor* at Whitchurch. A pity I chopped off the top arm on the left-hand signal! 'Bless 'em all!' (30 July 1963)

Above: Between Whitchurch and Shrewsbury a row of five withdrawn locos, two 'County' Class, two Class '2800' and a pannier tank, await movement to the scrapyard. The two workers on the rail trucks are making the most of the sunny weather with tops off – now they would have to roast with their hi-vis clothing on. (30 July 1963)

Above: One of 25 English Electric Type 4s that carried the names of ships owned either by Cunard, Elder Dempster or Canadian Pacific, this is No D230 *Scythia,* named after the liner that was part of the Cunard fleet from 1921 until 1958. The Type 4 is in the bay platform at Shrewsbury; nameplates were gradually removed from around 1970. (30 July 1963)

Above right: One of the crew of 'Hall' Class No 4964 *Rodwell Hall,* bereft of its smokebox door numberplate, adds the second lamp to upgrade it from a light engine to an express passenger, even though the stock looks nothing like an express passenger – it looks more like a parcels train!. (30 July 1963)

Right: Local 89A Shrewsbury 'Jubilee' Class No 45577 *Bengal* displays her nice clean lines as her train is loaded up with parcels. Bound for Birmingham and Paddington, she is standing next to 'blood and custard' stock forming part of the rake of the Shrewsbury to Paddington express ready to start the journey south. (30 July 1963)

Above left: 'Western' Class No D1005 *Western Venturer* pulls into Platform 4 at 2.26pm, 12 minutes late, with the 11.10am departure from Paddington, the 'Cambrian Coast Express'. The 'Western' will soon be uncoupled and a 'Manor' Class steam loco will be attached to the rear end of the train to take the right-hand curve towards Aberystwyth. Visible in the right background is the Abbey Church of St Peter and St Paul, which was founded in 1083. (30 July 1963)

Above: The 'Manors' were synonymous with the 'Cambrian Coast Express' on the Shrewsbury to Aberystwyth and Pwllheli sections, and here we have No 7818 *Granville Manor*, gleaming in the summer sunshine just about to leave at 2.42pm, a little late as the scheduled time was 2.28. According to the timetable she had 2 hours and 42 minutes to steam along the Cambrian line to Aberystwyth – no passports needed! Notice the external blanking door at the rear of the other train on the left. (30 July 1963)

Left: 'Warship' Class No D858 *Valorous* arrives at 2.33pm with the 8.00am Plymouth to Liverpool service. Not bad – only 11 minutes late after about 230 miles. (30 July 1963)

Left: Highlighting the trackwork around the southern end of the station is BR Standard 4MT No 80100, posing at the side of the 1902-constructed three-storey signal box – Severn Bridge Junction – which is now the largest remaining mechanical box on the network, although only about half of the 180 levers are still operational. (30 July 1963)

Ivatt Class 2MT 2-6-0 No 46510 has a low-sided tender and the coal bunker sides inset to allow for greater visibility when running in reverse. On this day she is employed on general shunting duties, having just passed about eight spotters at the end of Platform 4, obviously thinking that this was the best vantage point. (30 July 1963)

'Western' Class No D1059 *Western Empire* – only three months old – pulls into Platform 4 with the 11.05am through train from Swansea to Manchester. She will be uncoupled here and English Electric Type 4 No D340 will perform the final lap. It is noticeable that the spotters are wearing a more formal type of footwear, shoes rather than trainers, but none of them appear to be excited by the appearance of the three-month-old 'Western', so she is obviously not a cop. (30 July 1963)

English Electric Type 4 No D340 'whistles' as she 'ticks over' before departure to Manchester with the train from Swansea, on which she has just relieved No D1059. (30 July 1963)

'Hall' Class No 6916 *Misterton Hall* stands next to the Shrewsbury Town football supporters' score sign displaying either their last away win, 3-2 against Peterborough on 2 April 1963, or correctly predicting their win in the next local derby against Wrexham due to be played on Boxing Day 1963! (30 July 1963)

Named after the stately home in Norfolk, No 6934 *Beachamwell Hall* prepares for a short jaunt to Aberystwyth with a rake of eight coaches. Soon to be relieved of her Welsh connection, in three months she will be transferred to Banbury for a slightly different life before the end in 1965. (30 July 1963)

'Western' Class No D1006 *Western Stalwart* enters the station, with one of the floodlights from Gay Meadow, Shrewsbury FC's football ground, poking up above the trees. Mother, son and daughter in their Sunday best are maybe meeting someone; mother wears a cardigan and matching skirt with white high heels, daughter has white shoes and socks with her Sunday best dress and is holding an umbrella, and son has a white shirt, short trousers, white socks and black shoes, with a short back and sides haircut, and sucking a lollipop. Who are they meeting – grandparents, maybe? (30 July 1963)

At 3.40pm BR Standard Class 5 No 73070, with a mysterious smokebox inscription of '2K70'– a train reporting code perhaps – stands in the shadows with the sun shining on the top half of the vast array of advertising boards that were all along this long wall. The 'relax by rail' poster appears to be giving the message to park your car and do the rest by rail – was this the London Midland promoting an early option of Park and Ride? (30 July 1963)

There does not appear to be much urgency on Platform 2 to load parcels. I suppose 'Manor' Class No 7810 *Draycott Manor* is just content to wait until the driver moves the regulator. A 'whiskered' three-car Swindon-built Cross Country set waits at Platform 1 with the destination indicator showing Cardiff General, due to leave at 3.50pm. (30 July 1963)

5 • A week around Exeter

Exeter, the county town of Devon, stands on the River Exe, and was the most south-westerly Roman fortified settlement in Britain, with walls that still surround the city centre. According to the last Census in 2011, the ethnic composition was 93.1% white, with the largest minority ethnic group being Chinese at 1.7% (1,665); when I interrogated Trip Advisor I found that there are now many Chinese restaurants in the city, so I should probably revisit Exeter as that cuisine is high on my favourites list.

In 1961 on Edmund Street there was a three-storey-high, one-room-wide Tudor building that was threatened due to road development. It was decided not to demolish it but to put it on rollers and move it 70 metres to West Street beside St Mary Steps Church. It weighed 21 tonnes and was strapped together and moved a few inches at a time – a success.

There are three railway stations in Exeter– St David's, Central and the smaller St Thomas, which is now a Grade II-listed building. Exeter St David's has the distinction of being one of a few stations where you can travel to London by trains leaving in opposite directions; trains to Paddington leave northwards, but you can get to Waterloo by heading south, then turning eastwards just outside the station and being routed via Central.

'West Country' Class No 34107 *Blandford Forum* pulls out of the carriage sidings near Central station, passing the lineman who has his hands on the lever to reset the points. On the right can be seen the steep 1 in 37 gradient up from St David's station, with a multiple unit on its way down; the climb usually required banker assistance, and coupling the banker to a train on the descent was usual to cut down on light engine movements. On the left is the Anglican church of St Michael and All Angels, a relatively new church that was opened in 1868. (27 August 1963)

Leaving Exeter Central with the 12.30pm 'Atlantic Coast Express' service to Waterloo is 'Merchant Navy' Class No 35009 *Shaw Savill*, just passing Exeter Central A signal box. All this area has now been changed, with the signal box being removed and the track arrangement reduced and modified; the houses at the top of the banking have all disappeared to make way for a revamped B3183 road alignment scheme. (27 August 1963)

Left: 'West Country' Class No 34096 *Trevone* is just leaving Central with the 2.10pm 'Atlantic Coast Express' to Waterloo, after originating at Padstow at 11.00am. Padstow is only 2 miles from Trevone – a bit of a coincidence. (24 August 1963)

Below left: Off Exmouth Junction shed and 11 years old is BR Standard 3MT No 82001, bringing an on-time 2.11pm arrival into Central, being the 1.45pm local train from Exmouth. At the end of the year she would be transferred to Taunton, six months later to Barrow Road, then withdrawn six months later to be eventually broken up at Cashmore's, Newport, on 2 February 1966. (24 August 1963)

Right: 'Merchant Navy' Class No 35001 *Channel Packet* pulls in on one of the centre roads at 11.24am with the 8.00am departure from Surbiton, the Car Carrier Service to Okehampton. On the right is 'West Country' Class No 34002 *Salisbury* heading for Ilfracombe, and on the other centre road are a pair of 'W' Class 2-6-4Ts, Nos 31914 and 31924, awaiting the next banking duty. (24 August 1963)

Left: 'Merchant Navy' Class No 35001 *Channel Packet* was the prototype of the class, originally numbered 21C1 and built in 1941. 'Packet' refers to regularly scheduled cargo, passenger and mail ships, presumably operating across the Channel. (24 August 1963)

Below left: 'Merchant Navy' Class No 35016 *Elders Fyffes* arrives with the 11.00am departure from Waterloo, the 'Atlantic Coast Express'. The 2nd Class ordinary single fare from Waterloo to Exeter Central was advertised as 43 shillings (£2 3s), a little different from today's fares! The station cleaner on the extreme right, sitting down on the platform overbridge stairs, has brush in hand and at the ready, but is taking a break; he looks as if he is very close to retiring age, maybe even going before *Elders Fyffes* in two years time. Hopefully he had a dream and a plan for the rest of his life, just like Martin Luther King, who gave his 'I have a dream' speech the following day, calling for an end to racism and an improved quality of life for the black people of America – 'all men are created equal'. (27 August 1963)

Below right: These two locomotives had the honour of carrying the names and crests of two squadrons that saw action in both the First World War and the Battle of Britain in the Second World War. 'Battle of Britain' Class No 34080 *74 Squadron* and, behind, No 34072 *257 Squadron* move off together, maybe en route to the shed. On the extreme right are a man and woman, both standing still but obviously reading; it must be books or newspapers, as mobile phones and tablets were still in the 'that will never happen' phase! (24 August 1963)

Above: Another loco travelling light to the shed is 'Battle of Britain' Class No 34068 *Kenley*, named after RAF Kenley, a strategic airfield during the Battle of Britain; such was its importance that the Luftwaffe tried to destroy it in a bombing raid on 18 August 1940, but unsuccessfully as it was operational again the next day. (24 August 1963)

Above right: Of these two Ivatt 2MTs, No 41309 on the right is on freight duties, while No 41307 is taking the rear three coaches off the 'Atlantic Coast Express', which had arrived earlier behind No 35016 *Elder Fyffes*. (27 August 1963)

Right: BR Standard 4MT No 80035 storms out of Exeter Central with an unidentified train going east. (27 August 1963)

For about a year the 'W' Class tanks replaced the ailing 'Z' Class locomotives on banking duties, and here we have No 31915, enjoying a change with some shunting of various freight wagons. (27 August 1963)

Tranquillity, no movement, no hustle and bustle, just trees, hedging and calm conversation. The only sound is ex-LMS 2MT No 41318 maintaining pressure while standing in a rural-looking section of the large Central station. (27 August 1963)

'Merchant Navy' Class No 35030 *Elder Dempster Lines* has arrived 6 minutes late with the 11.15am service from Waterloo to Plymouth, now having the sound of its wheels checked by the wheeltapper before departure – might he have been singing the current Trini Lopez hit *If I Had a Hammer*? (24 August 1963)

Entering Central station and passing the two warning signs is 'Merchant Navy' Class No 35021 *New Zealand Line* with the 'Atlantic Coast Express', the 11.00am departure from Waterloo. Southern Region steam locomotives were by now few in number and were actually covered by Ian Allan in the October 1963 *abc Locoshed Book* on two pages – and that included the Isle of Wight locomotives! (24 August 1963)

Right: Crews were always happy to be in a shot, and you can see the proud expression of the driver even though his loco for the day is in a run-down condition, but he and his fireman are still in command of 'Battle of Britain' Class No 34079 *141 Squadron*. (27 August 1963)

The nameplate of 'Merchant Navy' Class No 35006 *Peninsular & Oriental S. N. Co.* included the Latin phrase 'Quis Nos Separabit', which was unique to P&O. Normally it would have been 'Quis Separabit' as on some military insignia and actually on some early P&O posters, but the company wanted a phrase that could be registered as the company's own by the College of Arms, so it included 'Nos', making the translation 'Who shall separate us'. (24 August 1963)

'Merchant Navy' Class No 35011 *General Steam Navigation* is on the approach road to Exmouth Junction shed, as viewed from our passing train to Exmouth, where we thought the shed was. However, as soon as we passed the 'Merchant Navy' all was revealed – Exmouth Junction Shed was in front of us at Exeter! Needless to say we got off at the first station and went back – schoolboy error! (24 August 1963)

'Battle of Britain' Class No 34060 25 *Squadron* coasts slowly down from Central and holds up the progress of two passenger trains outside the station in charge of which are Class '1400' No 1466 and 'Hall' Class No 6936 *Breccles Hall* coming from Exmouth and Newton Abbot respectively. (24 August 1963)

Left: Class '1400' No 1471 gives all that it's got to pull out of St David's with a two-coach train for Barnstaple and Ilfracombe. (24 August 1963)

Above: 'Battle of Britain' Class No 34083 *605 Squadron* attracts a group of Boy Scouts looking interested, and maybe gathering information hoping to gain their merit badge for railways/spotting! On the opposite platform is a traditional Wymans kiosk, a common feature of main-line stations, selling newspapers, books, magazines, sweets and tobacco; most written works are now viewed on websites, so what is the future for them? (24 August 1963)

Very dirty 'West Country' Class No 34020 *Seaton* enters St David's after coming down the 1 in 37 gradient from Central with the 1.49pm service from Salisbury, which will eventually find its way to Torrington. (24 August 1963)

Above left: 'Warship' Class No D822 *Hercules* brings in a service from Newton Abbot and passes two sets of signals; the right-hand one controlled movements of trains departing westward and that on the left was for trains reversing out of the up middle platform, both incorporating discs that were used in shunting operations. (24 August 1963)

Above: Class '2800' No 2886, on a Blue Circle Cement train from Westbury, is heading to the distribution facility near Exeter Central; this duty was usually the responsibility of a 'Hall' or a '2800'. The train is stationary waiting for two 'Z' Class bankers to be coupled at the rear. These 21 Presflo cement tanks are a very heavy load that could be upwards of 700 tonnes, so going up the 1 in 37 will be at walking pace. (24 August 1963)

Left: One of the Western Region's ubiquitous pannier tank locomotives, this one is Collett-designed Class '5700' No 4673. Both the loco and one of the crew are taking a rest on this hot, sunny afternoon. Gerry and the Pacemakers hit the pop scene in 1963, their first release being *How Do You Do It?*, then when everyone found out how to do it they released *I Like It!* (27 August 1963)

Above: A traditional comedian as well as a very good ballad singer, the young Ken Dodd was in the charts with *Still*, an apt song for this picture as time stands still on Platform 1 with Class '1400' No 1466 coupled to the usual two-coach train forming a Barnstaple service. The little boy's slightly flared black coat accentuates his sparrow-like legs. (24 August 1963)

Above right: Having waited for the 'all clear' (see page 74), 'Hall' Class No 6936 *Breccles Hall* enters St David's with the local from Newton Abbot, passing two observing spotters. (24 August 1963)

Right: 'Western' Class No D1068 *Western Reliance* pulls into Platform 2 with the 12.30pm service from Paddington to Plymouth, comprising 15 coaches – some effort, that, maybe with additional coaches as it was a busy summer Saturday. Although released earlier that year, people were still singing Cliff's *Summer Holiday* – it just made you feel good! (24 August 1963)

'Warship' Class No D847 *Strongbow* heads north with a train for York and, having arrived from the opposite direction, you can see a portion of the rake of 'The Cornishman' at the next platform, looking very full. I know diesel locomotives were relatively new, but it did seem that they were kept in pristine condition all of the time – well, that's what my photos proved. (24 August 1963)

One of Exmouth Junction's 'N' Class 2-6-0s, No 31840, on a very mixed goods, pauses on the middle road at St David's before attempting the incline to Central station with 'W' Class No 31912 at the rear for some genuine assistance. (29 August 1963)

'Hall' Class No 4932 *Hatherton Hall*, standing at Platform 2, will eventually take the right-hand fork out of St David's towards Newton Abbot with a service that has started from Taunton. Meanwhile 'Battle of Britain' Class No 34066 *Spitfire* will take the left-hand fork up the gradient to Central station. (29 August 1963)

Having been withdrawn on 17 November 1962 and having probably been in this position since then, Drummond Class '700' No 30689's days are well and truly over after 65 years service as she languishes at the western end of Tiverton Junction shed. (24 August 1963)

Right: Another old Drummond, having entered service in 1911, is Class 'M7' No 30125, and is another loco that had been withdrawn some two years earlier. Someone has chalked 'BUCK' and a face on the tanks – we will never know what the joke was or who it was intended for. (24 August 1963)

Below: Bringing up the rear on one of the two lines of withdrawn and dead locomotives at Tiverton Junction is 'Z' Class No 30951. A class of only eight, these 0-8-0 tank engines were all allocated to Exeter in 1959, employed on shunting and banking duties. (24 August 1963)

Below right: In the roofless Tiverton Junction shed is Class '4700' No 4706, one of the nine 'Night Owls' introduced in 1919. They were a Churchward design for heavy fast freight duties, but now, with the decline in freight workings, they were redeployed from the Old Oak area and some were used on passenger duties from Exeter along the Dawlish coast. (27 August 1963)

Off 83D Laira is 'Castle' Class No 7022 *Hereford Castle*, one of the last production batch of the class to emerge from Swindon only 14 years earlier; ironically in three months time she will be transferred to 86C Hereford, her 'home town'. (24 August 1963)

A class of 58 locos introduced in 1959 by the North British Locomotive Company of Glasgow (which went into voluntary liquidation in April 1962), these diesels were dubbed 'Baby Warships' and classified as Type 2. Here No D6318 approaches Yeoford with a train for Exeter. (29 August 1963)

Another North British Type 2, No D6319, arrives at Yeoford with the 11.55am Exeter Central to Plymouth service. On the left you can see an old gas lamp manufactured by Sugg, a company established in 1837 and still in existence today. The lamp had probably already been converted to electricity – you can see that it is missing its glass dome. (29 August 1963)

Having had her 'Spam can' casing removed in 1960, 'Battle of Britain' Class No 34060 *25 Squadron* off 72A Exmouth Junction storms through a deserted Yeoford station with an unidentified express. (29 August 1963)

BR Standard 4MT No 80037 trundles through Yeoford with a mixed freight. Just visible beyond the single-span footbridge is the road bridge, which was brick-built as two single arches spanning the two tracks. You really would not want to climb or descend the 'Way Out' stairs on the right, much steeper than those on the opposite side. ('Have you been involved in an accident recently…?' – injury claim at the ready!) (29 August 1963)

'Battle of Britain' Class No 34083 *605 Squadron* arrives at Yeoford at midday with the 10.30am Ilfracombe portion of the 'Atlantic Coast Express', due at Waterloo at 3.29pm, the only other stops being Exeter – to connect with and couple up other portions of the 'ACE' – and Salisbury. (29 August 1963)

6 • Reading, Didcot and Basingstoke

Similarities and connections between Reading, Didcot, and Basingstoke are few. You can basically categorise them as all towns, although Reading has recently made three failed attempts for city status and therefore still remains one of the largest urban areas in the UK without that privilege. They are all within the commuter belt for London with good road and rail connections, but having said that nowadays people's commuting mileage can be in excess of 150. Reading is noted for having hosted the Reading Festival since 1971, which takes place over the August bank holiday, and is, apart from Glastonbury, the largest pop festival in the UK.

Didcot is noted for its railway heritage. The Didcot Railway Centre, formed by the Great Western Society, is a site that retains many of the original GWR buildings housing the society's collection of preserved locomotives and rolling stock as well as being an engineering maintenance centre. Basingstoke is noted for Thomas Burberry, who was famous for inventing gabardine in 1879, a closely woven cloth used in the manufacture of raincoats and reinforcement in other garments.

Reading and Didcot are situated on the main rail route from the West and South Wales to London, with express services provided by InterCity 125's. This is very soon to change, with the completion of the first stage of electrification between London and Cardiff via Bristol Parkway, although the section from Bristol Parkway to Bristol Temple Meads has been deferred; without knowing the full implications and costs for just about 7 miles, this is hard for me to understand!

In 81D Reading is Class 9F No 92001, having come in with a freight from the Rugby area, its home shed; it has just been watered and is now ready for a return journey. (March 1964)

Class '9400' pannier tank No 8464 is parked up for the weekend with its next duties on Monday. Not too bad – a five-day week, but probably no annual holiday. It looks as though someone has been cleaning out a tender, leaving a few lumps but mainly coal dust that has collected at the bottom. (March 1964)

Below: One of the four 'Manor' Class 4-6-0s allocated to Reading at this time was No 7817 *Garsington Manor*, seen here standing in the bay platform on station pilot duty, ready for when called upon. There was a total solar eclipse on this day, with totality over the USA and Canada, but here in the south of the UK, nothing. (20 July 1963)

Above: 'Grange' Class No 6826 *Nannerth Grange* stands at the western end of the busy and full of steam nine-road 81D Reading shed, but life is to be short for the depot as it closed in January 1965 with its allocation transferred to Didcot, Southall and Worcester. (March 1964)

Above left: Class 'N' No 31859 is idle in the sidings near Reading South shed with two spotters sneaking round the shed and yards. All this area and the building skyline has changed beyond recognition, with the current electrification plan well in progress. (20 July 1963)

Above right: From the centre background to the foreground are St James's Church on Abbot's Walk; an assortment of buildings that have now been demolished and are now the route of the dual carriageway of Forbury Road; rows of empty coal wagons; Sulzer Type 3 No D6511; Class 'N' No 31871 moving onto the turntable at Reading South shed; then three covered wagons, one of which is displaying 'Earle's Cement', which must have been bagged and not ready-mixed. (20 July 1963)

Left: 'West Country' Class No 34037 *Clovelly* stands next to the corrugated-roofed cycle racks full of bikes at Reading South; this wasn't a fitness regime, but was the usual and almost obligatory form of transport to work. A sub-shed of 70C Guildford, this was a three-road, brick-built, straight-through shed. On the higher GWR tracks a 'Hymek' is doing some shunting of empty stock in the carriage siding, making more exhaust than a steam loco. (March 1964)

Above: The only thing in this picture that exists today is the track layout in the foreground. In the background are the *Reading Mercury* offices, Walter Parsons Corn Stores and Berkshire Waste, and even the modern-looking building has since been demolished. Reading South station (you can see the platform canopies) has gone, the carriages scrapped, Class '5700' No 4609 scrapped in 1965 and, judging by the age of the driver, I'm sure he too is no longer with us. Good job we've got photos!. (20 July 1963)

Above right: 'Modified Hall' No 7928 *Wolf Hall* approaches Reading at 2.06pm with the 1.15pm from Paddington to Worcester. On the right you can just see the end of one of the platforms of the South station next to the goods wagons. *Wolf Hall* was a rather unusual name for a stately home, but in fact it was Wulfhall in Burbage village, Wiltshire, which was the home of the Seymours at the time when Jane became Queen of England, having married Henry VIII to become his third wife of six. (20 July 1963)

Right: Pulling a rake of 12 coaches, 'Hall' Class No 6904 *Charfield Hall* approaches Reading with an express for Paddington; one of the crew is just happy to look at the camera while coasting into the platform. (20 July 1963)

Above: 'Hall' Class No 6960 *Raveningham Hall* poses in the middle road, with a Gloucester Railway Carriage & Wagon Company diesel multiple unit loading up with parcels before heading west. (20 July 1963)

Above right: Arriving at Reading at 1.39pm and already running 8 minutes late is 'Western' Class No D1016 *Western Gladiator* with the 12.45pm from Paddington to Bristol Temple Meads. (20 July 1963)

Right: 85A Worcester 'Castle' No 7023 *Penrice Castle* awaits departure at Reading at 1.28pm with a 13-coach train, the 10.05am from Hereford to Paddington, causing some interest from spotters. Buses parked in Station Square can be seen on the left; they also served passengers from Reading South station, as that terminus was also in the square. (20 July 1963)

The small 3,500-gallon tender of the 'Manor' Class is seen in close-up in this rear shot of No 7817 *Garsington Manor*. They were deliberately designed as the 'lightweights' of the Great Western's passenger fleet for cross-country and branch-line duties that the heavier 'Granges' were prohibited from working. Here she is on station pilot duties in the bay platform; I'm not sure what the metal frame is that is visible between the cab and tender. (20 July 1963)

Above: In the shed yards of Didcot is 'Grange' Class No 6853 *Morehampton Grange* with the chalked train identification '3X31'; this usually signified working an out-of-gauge load, but she is now resting for the weekend looking in good working order. She lasted until October 1965, and was then cut up at George Cohen Group's yard at Cransley, near Kettering. (March 1964)

Above right: Very clean-looking 9F No 92213 off 2D Banbury stands in Didcot shed yard, more than likely having brought in a coal train for Didcot Power Station. On the right is the avoiding line to Oxford. (March 1964)

Right: Seen from the northern end of Didcot shed, 'Hall' Class No 4905 *Barton Hall*, devoid of name and numberplates and having to endure a crude painted identification, stands near the brick and corrugated-iron structure of the single-road building in front of the main four-road shed. Two large chimneys have been attached to the boilers of two unlucky locomotives, their casings and innards being used as stationery boilers. (March 1964)

Diminutive Collett Class '1400' 0-4-2T No 1445 was built in 1935 and scrapped in 1965, having spent 30 years in service happily performing on local branch-line passenger trains. The class appears in the children's books and television series of *Thomas the Tank Engine*, and one also found film fame with a role in *The Titfield Thunderbolt*. (March 1964)

Above left: Steve McQueen, together with a host of other stars, was cast in *The Great Escape*, released a month earlier with classic music by Elmer Bernstein, which still plays out at some football grounds today, particularly if the team is in a relegation battle. However, there was no escape for Class '6100' No 6106, dead with sacking over the chimney; she was eventually withdrawn on 31 December 1965. (March 1964)

Above: Ian Dury and the Blockheads' *Reasons To Be Cheerful Part 3*, although not released until 1979, seems an apt title for this photo. With hands in pockets and jumping for joy at the cop of 'Western' Class No D1007 *Western Talisman*, my spotting friend John Charnock shows his delight as it passes through Didcot station. (March 1964)

Left: In this south-easterly view towards Reading and London, Brush Type 4 No D1684 with a relatively short rake enters Didcot. Her home shed was 2B Oxley, so it is possible she is heading towards Wolverhampton or Birmingham. (March 1964)

Class '6100' No 6136 is stationary on the curves outside the five-road shed of 81B Slough, which closed to steam on 1 January 1964. (20 July 1963)

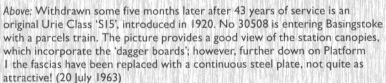

Above: Withdrawn some five months later after 43 years of service is an original Urie Class 'S15', introduced in 1920. No 30508 is entering Basingstoke with a parcels train. The picture provides a good view of the station canopies, which incorporate the 'dagger boards'; however, further down on Platform 1 the fascias have been replaced with a continuous steel plate, not quite as attractive! (20 July 1963)

Above right: 'N' Class No 31840 approaches Farnborough at 4.45pm with the Saturday 3.54pm Waterloo to Basingstoke service, passing a very nice rural property on Sturt Road, Frimley Green, that looks almost identical today, but worth a lot more no doubt. (20 July 1963)

Right: 'West Country' Class No 34031 *Torrington* arrives at Basingstoke with the 3.00pm Waterloo to Exeter service; the slight camber of the track is very noticeable. I'm not sure why there are two train identification numbers displayed on the front. (20 July 1963)

Maunsell 'U' Class 2-6-0 No 31615, with only three months to go before withdrawal, is seen in Brookwood sidings. Her build batch had slight detail differences from the original rebuilds from the 'River' Class that were introduced in 1917. (20 July 1963)

7 • Blackpool to Workington

Blackpool and Workington are both coastal towns, but like chalk and cheese. Blackpool on the Fylde Coast is the fun-loving glitzy tourist attraction and holiday resort with the Pleasure Beach, Tower, Tower Ballroom, trams and 7 miles of Illuminations along the Promenade. Heavily dependent on tourism, it went into a downward spiral in the 1960s with visitor numbers declining, mainly due to the popularity of package holidays to Spain. Over the years this has been addressed and now, with a population of 142,000 that is swelled weekly by an annual average in 2014 of 250,000 visitors, no wonder it is buzzing again. The Blackpool guest house landladies were at one time the butt of jokes by traditional stand-up comedians – you remember, they were the ones who actually told joke after joke, not like the modern ones, the life-relating bunch.

On the other hand, Workington is a quiet small town with a skyline that looks towards the Lake District fells with a population of 25,000. The original main employers, the coal and steel industries, were lost and the area became an unemployment black spot, from which it has never really recovered. The main employer now is out of town at the nuclear facility at Sellafield.

Above: Taken from the walking approach to 10B Blackpool, this view is looking north towards Blackpool Central with its vast array of semaphore signalling on the approaches to the station. The skyline is dominated by a tall chimney, the Tower and a gasometer; however, the nearer you get to the Tower, the more it wins 'hands down' for height. Just to the right but out of view is Bloomfield Road, Blackpool's football ground. (28 July 1964)

Left: 'Royal Scot' Class No 46160 *Queen Victoria's Rifleman* is seen with a recently fitted lamp complete with access ladder and an overhead crane – but why bother to airbrush them out? It was par for the course then, with telegraph poles, lamp standards, signals and water towers, and it's really no different today with all the overhead electrification equipment – you either take the photo or you don't! (28 July 1964)

Above: In the murky Blackpool South shed, with its extractors only having a partial effect, is 'Jubilee' Class No 45681 *Aboukir*. At weekends you could expect to see a full shed and yard with a mixture of locomotives from the Midland, Eastern and Scottish regions of the network having brought in seaside specials. The carriage sidings between the shed and Central station would also be full of empty stock waiting for the return journey. (28 July 1964)

Above right: In the 'North West Frontier' of the UK at Blackpool, one of the shed's own immaculate 'Jubilees', No 45584 *North West Frontier*, poses outside the shed. One of the coach parks for the seaside resort is just visible on the right, together with what looks like the new building of a multi-storey car park for the transportation that would bring about the decline of British Railways seaside specials in a couple of years time. (28 July 1964)

Right: 'Coronation' Class No 46228 *Duchess of Rutland* approaches Hest Bank and the only seaside stretch of line (about a mile) along the 401 miles it will have travelled with the Euston to Glasgow express. The camping coaches that are behind me at the end of the station platforms were to be my base for a week's spotting, together with about 40 other spotters, eight of whom can be seen on the bank on the right. We did not know each other but were bonded by a common cause. (25 July 1964)

After making a stop at Hest Bank, 'Britannia' Class No 70003 *John Bunyan* from Carlisle Kingmoor pulls away heading south. The typical lines of a BR Standard locomotive are in full view, and one of the crew wears a nice white cotton hat that will no doubt be black on completion of his shift later on. The mix of newish houses and bungalows along the skyline are on Marine Drive, but one stands out from the rest, being a much older large semi-detached property – the one above the dome of the 'Brit'; more than likely when the development was built this one already existed. (25 July 1964)

Above: Fifteen minutes later there was another 'Britannia', No 70024 *Vulcan*, from Crewe North with an 11-coach train. The 'Brits' given a new lease of life to the Midland lines – without that benefit they could well have been in the scrap-metal melting furnaces by now. (25 July 1964)

Above right: In Carnforth shed yards, for a freight engine 9F No 92046, off 8H Birkenhead, is very clean with painted buffers; she may have been recently outshopped from Crewe, although her final destination was to the South Wales scrapyard of Buttigieg's of Newport. (30 July 1964)

Right: Another loco in the yard was 'Jubilee' Class No 45606 *Falkland Islands* with no fixed abode, parked up and dead, smokebox door open, one front buffer missing – she's been in the wars, but little did she know that some 18 years later there really would be a war! Margaret Hilda Thatcher didn't pussyfoot about – nowadays she would probably have been a good ally for President Trump, both of them determined and outspoken! (30 July 1964)

Above: Outside the six-road straight-through shed at Carnforth stands 3F No 47468 with all features nicely identifiable. (30 July 1964)

Above right: Two 0-6-0s – one tank, one tender, 3F No 47317 and 4F 44386 respectively – are under the ash disposal plant, the tank exercising her seniority and getting in first. The seniority couldn't have been allocation, as they were both Carnforth locos; it couldn't have been age, as they were both built in 1924; so it must have been weight, the tank being 49½ tons and the tender loco 48¾ tons. (30 July 1964)

Right: In the 1945 film *Brief Encounter* with Celia Johnson and Trevor Howard, secretive station tearoom scenes were filmed at Carnforth station, and not 'Milford Junction' as portrayed in the film. 'Black Five' No 44697, with a self-weighing tender, has its own brief encounter, stopping only for a couple of minutes before departure to the north. After a few yards it will pass the old Midland signal box at the end of the opposite platform. (30 July 1964)

Above: 'Black Five' No 45336 stands outside the brick-built, ten-road, straight dead-ended shed at Barrow. For such an 'off the main route town', this was quite a large shed and in its heyday of the 1950s had an allocation of around 50 locos. (30 July 1964)

Above right: 4F No 44443 is idle for the weekend, but is in a fairly full Barrow shed of 31 locos, albeit that 13 were a mix of diesel shunters and Metropolitan-Vickers Type 2s; all 20 of the 'Metrovicks' were allocated to Barrow at that time. (30 July 1964)

Right: According to Martyn Bane, who is knowledgeable on Peckett industrial locomotives, this could be Peckett Class 'OY2' 0-4-0T Works No 2159 of May 1955, which was listed as having been sent to Barrow Iron Works. Here she is photographed in the docks yard of Vickers Ltd's Naval Construction Works, which was near the shed and next to the line over the wall by the semaphores. (30 July 1964)

The Bachelors were in the charts with a minor hit *Faraway Places* – well, 12D Workington shed was a faraway place on the west coast of England, with two 'Black Fives', Nos 45054 and 45294, both from Carnforth, having a rest outside the dead-ended shed, whose allocation was predominantly for freight workings. (30 July 1964)

8 • Lancashire

There are two areas in the UK where the round and the funny ball – soccer and Rugby League – divide communities. One is Yorkshire and the other is Lancashire. In Lancashire, for Rugby League you have St Helens, Widnes, Wigan and Warrington as the main contenders, and for football it's Liverpool, Everton, Blackburn, Bolton, Preston and Burnley. A large percentage of the population only actively follow one sport, with both sets of supporters until the 1960s being of the 'cloth cap' brigade with wooden rattles, then fashions changed slightly and they became 'bobble-hatted' and banner-waving.

The main industry in Lancashire was cotton, with many mills, so it is no wonder that the four main inventors in the industry were all from Lancashire: John Kay (flying shuttle), Richard Arkwright (spinning frame), Samuel Crompton (spinning mule), and James Hargreaves (spinning jenny). When you think of cotton you immediately think of the tall chimneys of the mills that were the backdrop of the 'matchstick men' paintings of L. S. Lowry, and Fred Dibnah, the Bolton steeplejack, who felled most of them with his own unique style of demolition aided by timber and fire.

There was a dense network of railway lines in Lancashire resulting in many sheds, and as a consequence railways must have been a major employer in the area; however, as with the cotton industry that has now declined, and in the words of the song by the American rock band Clutch, 'You can't stop progress.'

The Animals had a 1964 hit with *The House of the Rising Sun* – is this it? 'Coronation' Class No 46243 *City of Lancaster* catches the sun in 8A Edge Hill shed, with two patches on her 'blinker' – they will shortly disappear, but soon she will have one permanent stripe on her cabside identifying her as banned from under the electrification wires south of Crewe. (28 July 1964)

Above: Liverpool FC were now a recognised force after winning promotion to the First Division in 1962 and in the 1964 season winning the League for the first time in 17 years. Support divides the city – while there is nobody in the picture you can bet that half of them have allegiance to 'the Reds'! Standing outside the main Liverpool shed of Edge Hill is 5MT No 45187. You would have thought that soon she would succumb to the overhead wires and be replaced by an electric, but no – she went on nearly to the end, being withdrawn June 1968. (28 July 1964)

Above right: Standing between the turntable and the overhead coal loader at Edge Hill is 'Crab' No 42815. She's bound to know where everything is because this has been her home shed for the last couple of years, but unfortunately the end was near within two months, being withdrawn in September. (28 July 1964)

Right: All the way from 2J Aston is 'Britannia' Class No 70029 *Shooting Star*, but not looking as bright as a meteorite, running light engine on the main lines adjacent to Warrington Dallam shed. We had seen her a couple of hours earlier in Wigan Springs Branch. (28 July 1964)

Above: The Rolling Stones were at No 1 in the charts with *It's All Over Now*, and that was the story for the 'Coronation' Class on the named trains! Here you see one of their successors, English Electric Type 4 No D325, speeding through Warrington and displaying the 1M20 headcode for 'The Caledonian', which left Glasgow Central at 8.30am for Euston. Another practice that was over, or gradually disappearing, was the use of named train headboards, although the name of the service was still placed on the carriage boards. (28 July 1964)

Right: Built at Derby and introduced in 1932 is Fowler 4MT No 42378, seen here in the yard at Warrington Dallam but in nine months it would be withdrawn and scrapped at Central Wagon Co, Ince, Wigan. (28 July 1964)

Right: Here I am at Wigan – 'Who Ate All The Pies'. It's Springs Branch with an allocation of about 60, so it was surprising for me to find 66 engines on shed, copping 47 of them. One was 3F No 47671, parked over the ash/inspection pits outside the shed. Typically on the right you can see the northern style of terraced houses, rows of which were interconnected by 'ginnels', or alleyways, as typified in *Coronation Street*, which was now in its fourth year and attracting 20 million regular viewers. But then we only had three channels to watch, so it was basically *Coronation Street* or nothing. (28 July 1964)

Above: 5MT No 44741, with Caprotti valve gear, stands in the open yards of Speke. The track on the left curved round to eventually form a triangle of lines, and on the right you can just make out carriages in the sidings. (28 July 1964)

Right: Many enthusiasts considered the 1947 Ivatt 4MT 2-6-0 as the ugliest British locomotive ever produced, but it's a matter of opinion. The contentious area was the high positioning of the running plate, which exposed most of the workings, but some four years later the British Railways Standard designs were adopted, which also had high running plates and were considered elegant, so what's the problem? Here No 43033 off Heaton Mersey poses under the wires at Speke waiting for the next call of duty. (28 July 1964)

Above: Both driver and fireman pose nonchalantly in the cab of unusually clean 8F 2-8-0 No 48294 at Speke, with another 2-8-0 behind, but not quite the same as it's a 'WD'. There were similarities, except one – the 8Fs' motion didn't 'clank' when running! (28 July 1964).

Left: South Africa, and particularly the Battle of Rorke's Drift between the British Army and the Zulus, was featured in the 1964 film *Zulu*, which elevated Michael Caine – taking his first major role – to stardom. There is a bit of a 'drift' in front of 'Jubilee' Class No 45571 *South Africa* here at 8C Speke Junction, but it's rubble and ash, nothing worth fighting over and certainly nothing that would constitute a battle – nobody really cared any more. (28 July 1964)

Right: Bank Hall shed at Liverpool was situated in the Bootle area of the city, sandwiched between Canada Docks to the west and Everton's Goodison Park ground to the east, both being noted for their strikers, but for entirely different reasons. There are no dockers or footballers in sight here, only 23 engines, one of which was 5MT No 44929. (28 July 1964)

Below right: On Grand National Day, Aintree shed would be overflowing with locos having brought in specials from all over the country, their passengers then witnessing the most famous steeplechase in the world, horses and jockeys completing two laps of the left-handed course for the trophy. This year's winner was Team Spirit at 18 to 1. That was longer than the 2 to 1 odds offered for spotting a Class 'WD' on shed – in the eight-road dead-ended building and yard I spotted 19 locos, 10 of which were 'WDs'. Here we see No 90712 on shunting duties on the main line adjacent to the shed. (28 July 1964)

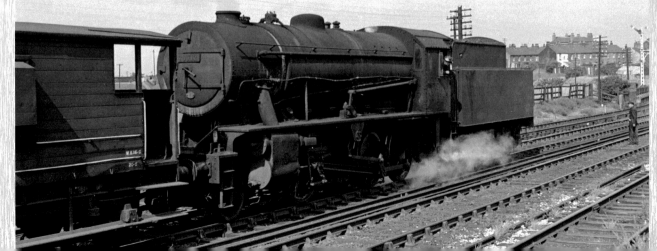

Above: 5MT No 45330 stands next to the coal stage and the water storage building at Aintree, with its smokebox door open and the cleaner with what looks like his ash rake ready for action. The 'Black Five' looks as if she is at maximum pressure, so rather him than me!. (28 July 1964)

9 • Edinburgh area

A couple of hundred years ago the traditional industries in Edinburgh were printing, brewing and distilling, but during the 20th century they have been overshadowed by banking, insurance and the investment sector to such an extent that it is now only second to London as a UK financial centre. Tourism is also of great economical importance to the city, and indeed Scotland, with Edinburgh being the second most visited, again after London. Boasting four universities, I suppose it is similar to Oxford and Cambridge, with large numbers of students in relatively small cities. In terms of sport, and in particular football, the teams of Heart of Midlothian and Hibernian mostly play second fiddle to Celtic and Rangers of Glasgow, which have dominated the sport up there for so long.

For spotting Sassenachs, this area's sheds instilled you with high expectations in terms of 'cops'. With the exception of some of their 'Pacifics', not much else of their allocation came to us south of the border – it was unknown territory, and I was about to reap the rewards for the effort of an overnight journey.

These two Class 'A3s', Nos 60077 *The White Knight* and 60042 *Singapore*, were named after the winners of the 1907 and 1908 Ascot Gold Cup and the 1930 St Leger respectively. However, they are not looking like thoroughbreds here, standing forlornly in a line of dead locos at St Margarets. I don't think they ever moved again, both having been withdrawn on the same day, 13 July 1964, and both cut up at Arnott Young of Carmyle in October. (26 July 1964)

Above: Outside at St Margarets is Class 'A1' No 60129 *Guy Mannering*, named after the anonymously published Walter Scott novel of 1815. She was one of a few 'Pacifics' allocated to 52D Tweedmouth, just south of the Scottish border, primarily for main-line 'standby' duties. (26 July 1964)

Above right: Class 'B1' No 61191 stands on one of the two ash pit roads at St Margarets; you can see in the foreground one of the water taps that were installed along the pits, to which hoses could be connected to douse the hot ashes. (26 July 1964)

Right: The Gresley 'V2' 2-6-2 tender engines were built over a six-year period from 1936 for express mixed-traffic workings. This example, No 60813, was fitted with a stovepipe chimney and small smoke deflectors, but still retained its three cylinders in the original monoblock arrangement. Here she is on the south side of St Margarets shed at the extreme end next to the flats on Restalrig Road North, whose residents were not fans of the depot due to excessive smoke and noise, although it was a bit better for them now as most of the engines in that area were dead. (26 July 1964)

Below: A Scottish-based freight and short-distance mineral-haulage workhorse, Class 'J38' No 65915 simmers at St Margarets, her home shed. These engines were mainly used for transportation of coal from the Lothian and Fife mines, and although a perceivably dirty duty there is not much trace of grime. (26 July 1964)

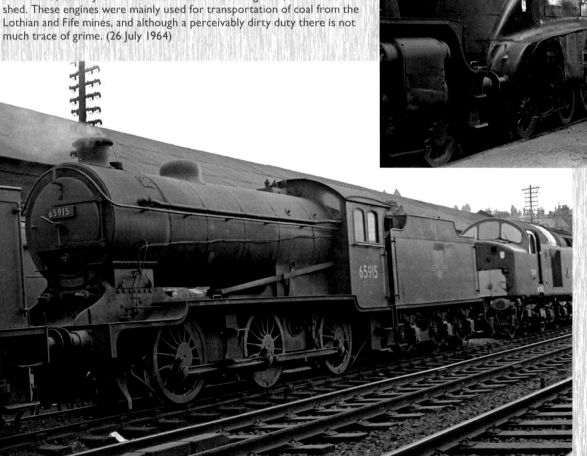

Above: Light being reflected off her casing, she's probably reflecting on her career as a Gateshead engine for all of her 26 years of running, and looking in exceptional condition for someone living at that shed, which did not have a reputation for cleanliness! Class 'A4' No 60001, named after Sir Ronald Matthews, who was Chairman of the London & North Eastern Railway and had been Master Cutler in Sheffield, is inside the main St Margarets six-road, dead-ended shed. On the roads outside there are plenty of live steam engines. (26 July 1964)

Left: In a run-down Haymarket shed, once the bastion of Scottish 'Pacifics', our hearts sank as there was nothing to be seen but diesels. On view here are English Electric Type 4 No D264 with 'Deltic' No D9016 *Gordon Highlander* and an unidentified sister loco. (26 July 1964)

Right: After manoeuvring out of the 'line-up' and backing onto a Clayton diesel on the dead-end road, here is a better view of 'Deltic' No D9016 *Gordon Highlander*. The Gordon Highlanders were formed in 1794 and survived for 200 years before being amalgamated with The Queen's Own Highlanders. No D9016 was in immaculate condition in preparation for being officially named at Aberdeen two days later; between 1999 and 2003 she was the only 'Deltic' to have a black background applied to her nameplates, which was when the loco carried the Porterbrook livery. (26 July 1964)

Above: Class 'A3' No 60098 *Spion Kop* conjures up evocative memories for me as a season ticket holder for Sheffield Wednesday's 'Spion Kop' in the early 1960s. The ground regularly held 50,000 supporters, and on occasions was filled to capacity with 65,000, the majority standing. Some 50-odd years later I still go and see them, getting tickets for behind the goal – my favourite spot. Stadiums are now all-seated, but we still stand up! Food for thought for the FA, but still with safety in mind? (30 November 1963)

Left: A long line of Scottish 'Pacifics' await their fate – although minds have already been made up for the thousands of tons of steel at Bathgate. (30 November 1963)

Above: A sobriquet for the city of Perth, *Saint Johnstoun*, Class 'A1' No 60162, had been condemned on 28 October 1963 so was really a new arrival to Bathgate, and was still named – but for how long? You can see some of our spotting group, all with coats on as the temperature was just about freezing with a damp mist. (30 November 1963)

Above right: The Midland and Western regions had their highly successful two-cylinder mixed-traffic 4-6-0s, the 'Black Fives' and 'Halls' respectively, while the 'B1' was the Eastern Region's counterpart. Here we have No 61238 *Leslie Runciman*, one of 59 of the 410 'B1s' to be named, this one in honour of a Newcastle ship-owner. (30 November 1963)

Right: It seemed that there were a lot of 0-6-0s around that were very old, and members of classes I had never seen before. Here is a Macintosh Caledonian 3F No 57550, introduced in 1899, which to put it in perspective was nearing the end of Queen Victoria's reign. Withdrawn on 29 December 1962, she did hang around dead until June 1964, when she was cut up at Arnott Young. (30 November 1963)

Above: Class 'A3' No 60099 *Call Boy* has a ragged chimney but still carries her name and numberplate, giving her the faintest hope of recovery – diesels might fail if there is a hard winter, and fires might be lit again – but it proved to be a false hope. (30 November 1963)

Above right: Lines from Shirley Bassey's 1963 hit *I (Who Have Nothing)* have parallels with the state of Peppercorn 'A2' No 60537, her nameplates conspicuous by their absence, but still a 'namer' to us, *Bachelor's Button*, albeit never to move again. The houses on Edinburgh Road in the background all appear to have curtains and blinds at the windows – maybe in the depths of the northern winters they help to keep them just a little warmer. (30 November 1963)

Right: Introduced in 1910, Class 'N15' 0-6-2 tank No 69211, with spyglass windows, had been withdrawn the year before but was still visually in 'good nick'. I think it stood there for another six months, as it wasn't cut up at McLellans until June 1964. (30 November 1963)

Below:: Most of the locos at Bathgate during this period were dead, stored and waiting for a scrap buyer. Among them was Class 'V2' No 60892. It had only been a few years ago when I started trainspotting that these Eastern Region mixed-traffic locos, some green, some in black livery, were thundering up the lines on passenger, freight and fish trains in all their glory, a powerful and well-loved class. (30 November 1963)

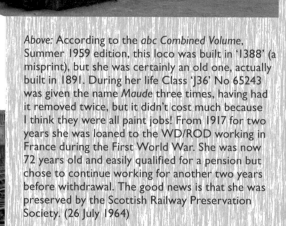

Above: According to the *abc Combined Volume*, Summer 1959 edition, this loco was built in '1388' (a misprint), but she was certainly an old one, actually built in 1891. During her life Class 'J36' No 65243 was given the name *Maude* three times, having had it removed twice, but it didn't cost much because I think they were all paint jobs! From 1917 for two years she was loaned to the WD/ROD working in France during the First World War. She was now 72 years old and easily qualified for a pension but chose to continue working for another two years before withdrawal. The good news is that she was preserved by the Scottish Railway Preservation Society. (26 July 1964)

Right: The 'J37s' were designed by Reid and built between 1914 and 1920. No 64614 was one of the class of 104 engines, latterly all based in Scotland. She is displaying a St Margarets shedplate but was actually based at Polmont – probably there were no 64E plates left – 'computer says no'! (26 July 1964)

Left: This class had previously eluded me. 'J83' No 68477, designed by Holmes and built in 1900 – another Victorian – had been withdrawn in December 1962. She may have been in Bathgate for about a year, so had she seized up? As Chuck Berry said, *No Particular Place To Go…* (26 July 1964)

Right: Class 'B1' No 61308 is at Dalry Road next to pile of what looks like brake blocks. An unidentified 0-4-0 diesel shunter is on the right. (26 July 1964)

Class 'B1' No 61307 is also seen at Dalry Road; based at St Margarets, she was soon to transfer here to 64C. She is standing next to a load of drums, the one in the foreground marked 'petroleum', with me standing next to them taking the photo – it would not be allowed nowadays. The main line to Princes Street, Edinburgh, can be seen on the right. (26 July 1964)

Index

Silver Link Silk Editions

In March 2014 we introduced the first of our Silver Link Silk Editions, which will feature a silver, gold or green silk style bookmark (the use of such silks dates back to the reign of Elizabeth 1). Printed on high quality gloss art paper, these sewn hardcover volumes also feature head and tail bands. Such quality and tradition will be much welcomed by today's discerning print book readers.

Further Silk Edition volumes will be made available from time to time and details will be shown on our web site: www.nostalgiacollection.com

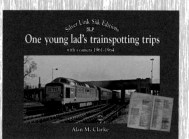

Further information

Silver Link and Past & Present titles are available while stocks last through bookshops, preserved railways and many heritage sites throughout the UK.

Further details can be found on our web site:
www.nostalgiacollection.com

Our latest catalogue is also available on request by writing to us at the address shown on the title page of this volume or by emailing your request to:

silverlinkpublishing@btconnect.com

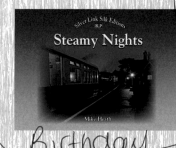

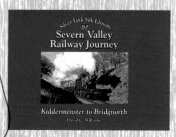

Birthday ♡